RADICAL DIS

CW00746253

A course for new Christians

Paul Beasley-Murray

CONTENTS

Introduction

INTRODUCTION

The Great Commission

Just before he ascended to his Father, the risen Lord Jesus gave what the Duke of Wellington once called 'the marching orders of the church'. Here in the Great Commission is to be found the basis of this course for new Christians.

Matthew 28:18-20 Jesus said, "All authority in heaven and on earth has been given to me. Therefore go and make disciples of all nations, baptising them in the name of the Father and of the Son and of the Holy Spirit, and teaching them to obey everything I have commanded you. And surely I am with you always, to the very end of the age."

A call to discipleship

As Christians we are called to be '*disciples*', ie we are called to be followers of the Lord Jesus, committing ourselves to him not only in baptism but also in the ongoing task of going Christ's way. It is not without significance that in the New Testament the term 'Christian' is only found three times, whereas the term 'disciple' is used 269 times. The former term is just a label, whereas the latter term contains a sense of movement and direction. As disciples of the Lord Jesus we never 'graduate' from his school - we are always learning from him, we are always dependent on him. Baptism does not mark the end of the process of becoming a Christian - it simply marks the end of the beginning!

A call to radical discipleship

Radical disciples are those who root their lives in Jesus and in God's Word, the Bible. The word '*radical*' comes from the Latin '*radix*', which means 'root'. In this baptismal course we will see how the Baptist understanding of Christian discipleship is rooted in scripture. Indeed, the approach adopted by this course is to encourage people to think about ten different aspects of discipleship by examining in depth a limited number of scripture passages all grouped together under one common theme. Furthermore, recognising that many people today cannot easily find their way through the Bible, every scripture passage to which reference is made is reproduced in full - in the New International Version of the Bible.

A word to the course leader

You will notice that the comments introducing each passage of scripture are limited. In one sense this creates more work for the course leader, for inevitably these comments need expansion. Yet the limited nature of these comments actually makes it easier to use this course with people of very different backgrounds and of quite different ages. A useful reference book for the course leader is *Radical Believers: the Baptist way of being the church* (Baptist Union of Great Britain 1992) by Paul Beasley-Murray. The Baptist Union video *Baptist Basics* might also be used with profit.

RESPONDING TO CHRIST

Christian basics

Here we have one of the earliest Christian creeds - possibly learnt by Paul when he too was preparing for baptism. The death and resurrection of Jesus are at the heart of the Christian faith. Notice how the death of Jesus is 'for our sins'.

1 Corinthians 15:3-5 **For what I received I passed on to you as of first importance: that Christ died for our sins according to the Scriptures, that he was buried, that he was raised on the third day according to the Scriptures, and that he appeared to Peter, and then to the Twelve.**

Repenting

Repentance is the first step in becoming a Christian. Repentance always involves a change of direction - it is not just a feeling sorry, but an actual turning away from sin, and instead going the way of Jesus.

Acts 2:37-38 **When the people heard this, they were cut to the heart and said to Peter and the other apostles, "Brothers, what shall we do?" Peter replied, "Repent and be baptised, every one of you, in the name of Jesus Christ for the forgiveness of your sins. And you will receive the gift of the Holy Spirit."**

Believing

The second step in becoming a Christian is believing in God's love for us. It is almost incredible that God should love us all so much that he should give his Son. It is also almost incredible that God's offer of life is open to all who believe - as distinct from just those who in one way or another might be deemed to deserve his life.

John 3:16 **For God so loved the world that he gave his one and only Son, that whoever believes in him shall not perish but have eternal life.**

Surrendering

Romans 10:9 **If you confess with your mouth, "Jesus is Lord," and believe in your heart that God raised him from the dead, you will be saved.**

Believing is more than an act of the mind, it also an act of will. Christians are not free agents - they have surrendered themselves to the service of Jesus. Jesus is to be not just our Saviour - he is also to be our Lord.

Receiving

Romans 8:9-17 **If anyone does not have the Spirit of Christ, he does not belong to Christ ... And if the Spirit of him who raised Jesus from the dead is living in you, he who raised Christ from the dead will also give life to your mortal bodies through his Spirit, who lives in you ... You received the Spirit of sonship. And by him we cry, "*Abba*, Father." The Spirit himself testifies with our spirit that we are God's children. Now if we are children, then we are heirs - heirs of God and co-heirs with Christ, if indeed we share in his sufferings in order that we may also share in his glory.**

As we in faith give ourselves to God, God in his turn gives himself to us. He gives himself to us in sending his Spirit. It is the Holy Spirit who makes God real in our lives and satisfies our spiritual hunger. We were made to relate with God - now we have become what we were intended to be.

Following

Mark 8:34-36 **Then he called the crowd to him along with his disciples and said: "If anyone would come after me, he must deny himself and take up his**

Jesus never pretended the Christian life was easy. There is a cost - no life of our own! For when Jesus calls us to 'take up our cross' he calls us to go the way of death. Following

Jesus involves more than easy 'believism' - it involves a commitment of a lifetime.

cross and follow me. For whoever wants to save his life will lose it, but whoever loses his life for me and for the gospel will save it. What good is it for a man to gain the whole world, yet forfeit his soul?"

Memory verse: John 3:16

NB If we are to be effective Christians we need to programme our minds, just as a computer is only effective as it's 'memory' is programmed. Hence at the end of each section, a memory verse is suggested.

PS If you wish to go the 'extra mile', there is much to be said for learning off by heart the order of the books of the Bible. Start with the New Testament; go on to Genesis-Psalms, and finish with Proverbs-Malachi. The benefit, of course, is that you will be able to find your way through the Bible so much more easily.

OBEYING CHRIST

The command of Christ

Matthew 28:18-20 **Then Jesus came to them and said, "All authority in heaven and on earth has been given to me. Therefore go and make disciples of all nations, baptising them in the name of the Father and of the Son and of the Holy Spirit, and teaching them to obey every-thing I have commanded you. And surely I am with you al-ways, to the very end of the age."**

Baptism is no optional extra. Jesus expects his disciples to commit themselves to him in the waters of baptism. Baptism is part of the normal Christian life.

The example of Christ

Matthew 3:13-17 **Then Jesus came from Galilee to the Jordan to be baptised by John. But John tried to deter him, saying, "I need to be baptised by you, and do you come to me?" Jesus replied, "Let it be so now; it is proper for us to do this to fulfil all righteousness." Then John consented. As soon as Jesus was baptised, he went up out of the water. At that moment heaven was opened, and he saw the Spirit of God descending like a dove and lighting on him. And a voice from heaven said, "This is my Son, whom I love; with him I am well pleased."**

Although there are differences between the baptism of Jesus and ours, nonetheless like Jesus we must be prepared to submit ourselves to the will of God and 'do what God requires' (GNB). Like Jesus we must be obedient.

The practise of the early church

In New Testament times there was no such person as an unbaptised Christian. Baptism was part of the process of becoming a Christian.

Acts 2:37-38 **When the people heard this, they were cut to the heart and said to Peter and the other apostles, "Brothers, what shall we do?" Peter replied, "Repent and be baptised, every one of you, in the name of Jesus Christ for the forgiveness of your sins. And you will receive the gift of the Holy Spirit."**

A declaration of union with Christ

Baptism is a dramatic way of declaring our solidarity with Jesus, crucified and risen. In this 'watery grave' we resolve to die to self and to live for Christ.

Romans 6:3-4 **Don't you know that all of us who were baptised into Christ Jesus were baptised into his death? We were therefore buried with him through baptism into death in order that, just as Christ was raised from the dead through the glory of the Father, we too may live a new life.**

A sign of cleansing

In baptism we acknowledge that we are sinners who stand in need of Christ's cleansing power. In this 'bath' our sins are washed away as we commit ourselves to the Christ who died for us.

Acts 22:16 **"And now what are you waiting for? Get up, be baptised and wash your sins away, calling on his name."**

A confession of faith

Baptism is the moment when we nail our colours to the mast and publicly

1 Timothy 6:12 **Fight the good fight of the faith. Take hold of**

the eternal life to which you were called when you made your good confession in the presence of many witnesses.

1 Corinthians 12:13 **For we were all baptised by one Spirit into one body - whether Jews or Greeks, slave or free - and we were all given the one Spirit to drink.**

Ephesians 1:13-14 **And you also were included in Christ when you heard the word of truth, the gospel of your salvation. Having believed, you were marked in him with a seal, the promised Holy Spirit, who is a deposit guaranteeing our inheritance until the redemption of those who are God's possession - to the praise of his glory.**

declare in front of others that we belong to Jesus and to his people. Hence the need to ensure that we bring along a good number of friends when we are baptised.

A rite of initiation

Baptism is the normal way of entering the church. We are baptised into the body of Christ. Hence church membership is an integral part of baptism. To commit ourselves to Jesus involves committing ourselves to the people of Jesus.

A sign of the Spirit's presence

The Spirit is God's gift to all who put their trust in Jesus. Not surprisingly baptism, where we express our trust in Jesus, is often associated with the gift of God's Spirit. See also Matthew 3:13-17, Acts 2:38 and 1 Corinthians 12:13.

Memory verses: Matthew 28:18-20

9

GROWING IN CHRIST

Growing up in the family

We need the company of other Christians. For we will only grow into maturity as we receive both encouragement and discipline from within the family of Christ.

Ephesians 4:14-16 **Then we will no longer be infants, tossed back and forth by the waves, and blown here and there by every wind of teaching and by the cunning and craftiness of men in their deceitful scheming. Instead, speaking the truth in love, we will in all things grow up into him who is the Head, that is, Christ. From him the whole body, joined and held together by every supporting ligament, grows and builds itself up in love, as each part does its work.**

Feeding on God's Word

We need too to develop a system of daily Bible reading. We need to feed our minds as also our spirits on God's word. Only so will we grow.

1 Peter 2:2 **Like newborn babies, crave pure spiritual milk, so that by it you may grow up in your salvation.**

Learning from God's Word

The Bible is to be trusted - for God has wonderfully 'inspired' men and women to tell the story of his saving acts. The teaching found within the Bible is also to be obeyed - for here is God's pattern for our life together.

2 Timothy 3:15 **The holy Scriptures ... are able to make you wise for salvation through faith in Christ Jesus. All Scripture is God-breathed and is useful for teaching, rebuking, correcting and training in righteousness, so** that the man of God may be thoroughly equipped for every good work.

Learning to pray

Matthew 7:7, 9-11 "Ask and it will be given to you; seek and you will find; knock and the door will be opened to you ... Which of you, if his son asks for bread, will give him a stone? Or if he asks for a fish, will give him a snake? If you, then, though you are evil, know how to give good gifts to your children, how much more will your Father in heaven give good gifts to those who ask him!"

As we begin to grow, we learn to speak - and listen - to God in prayer. Our heavenly Father delights in his children bringing to him their concerns.

Submitting to the Father's will

Luke 22:42 "Father, if you are willing, take this cup from me; yet not my will, but yours be done."

As we grow we discover that sometimes God says 'no' to our prayers. Sometimes this is for our own good - sometimes it is for the good of others. Although at the time we may not understand why our prayers are not answered in the way we wish, we can always trust God that his ways are best.

Living in Christ

John 15:4-5 "Remain in me, and I will remain in you. No branch can bear fruit by itself; it must remain in the vine. Neither can you bear fruit unless you remain in me. I am the vine; you

It is in our ongoing developing relationship with Jesus that we find the strength for daily living. Our own resources are limited. Much as we wish to be active in Christ's service, our activism must be balanced by times of quiet resting in Jesus.

Making time for God

If Jesus found it necessary to make time - and space! - for God, then surely it must be even more true of us. All of us need to find time within the busyness of our lives to 'centre down' and discover God's direction and strength for our lives.

are the branches. If a man remains in me and I in him, he will bear much fruit; apart from me you can do nothing."

Mark 1:35 **Very early in the morning, while it was still dark, Jesus got up, left the house and went off to a solitary place, where he prayed.**

Memory verses: John 15:4-5

FOLLOWING CHRIST

Getting our priorities straight

Matthew 6:33 "Seek first his [God's] kingdom and his righteousness, and all these things will be given to you as well."

A hallmark of Christian discipleship is that God comes first in our lives. Jesus promises that God will look after the needs of those who are concerned above everything else to do what he requires.

Producing fruit

Galatians 5:22-25 The fruit of the Spirit is love, joy, peace, patience, kindness, goodness, faithfulness, gentleness and self-control ... Those who belong to Christ Jesus have crucified the sinful nature with its passions and desires. Since we live by the Spirit, let us keep in step with the Spirit.

Another hallmark of Christian discipleship is that we reflect the Lord Jesus in the kind of people we are. This comes about as we seek to allow his Spirit to have control of our lives.

Forgiving our enemies

Matthew 6:14-15 For if you forgive men when they sin against you, your heavenly Father will also forgive you. But if you do not forgive men their sins, your Father will not forgive your sins.

To reflect the Lord Jesus in our lives means that we will forgive those who have hurt us. Forgiveness does not mean minimising the wrong done; it means letting go of our feelings of anger and bitterness.

Going against the stream

Romans 12:2 Do not conform any longer to the pattern of this

It's not easy following Christ. Whether it be in our relationships with the opposite sex or in the way in which we conduct ourselves at work, our values are different. It takes courage to go the way of Jesus.

Discovering God's will

The Spirit guides us in various ways - through scripture, through circumstances, through reasoning, through the advice of Christians friends, as also through inner promptings.

Dealing with temptation

There can be no room for complacency - temptation is inevitable when we are seeking to follow the Lord Jesus. Giving in to temptation, however, need not be inevitable!

Dealing with failure

There are times when we fail Christ - and fail one another. But, however badly we may have failed, in Jesus there is always a new beginning.

world, but be transformed by the renewing of your mind. Then you will be able to test and approve what God's will is - his good, pleasing and perfect will.

Acts 16:9-10 During the night Paul had a vision of a man of Macedonia standing and begging him, "Come over to Macedonia and help us." After Paul had seen the vision, we got ready at once to leave for Macedonia, concluding that God had called us to preach the gospel to them.

1 Corinthians 10:12-13 If you think you are standing firm, be careful that you don't fall! No temptation has seized you except what is common to man. And God is faithful; he will not let you be tempted beyond what you can bear. But when you are tempted, he will also provide a way out so that you can stand up under it.

1 John 1:7-9 The blood of Jesus, his Son, purifies us from all sin ... If we confess our sins, he is faithful and just and will

forgive us our sins and purify us from all unrighteousness.

When we have fallen in the race of faith, he allows us, as it were, to pick up ourselves and continue from where we fell.

Memory verse: Matthew 6:33

WORSHIPPING CHRIST

Giving God the glory

Worship is the occasion when we acknowledge God's 'worth'. Christian worship in particular centres on the new thing that God has done in Jesus. Sunday by Sunday we come to celebrate the resurrection of the Crucified.

Psalm 96:1-3 **Sing to the Lord a new song; sing to the Lord, all the earth. Sing to the Lord, praise his name; proclaim his salvation day after day. Declare his glory among the nations, his marvellous deeds among all peoples.**

Listening to God speak

Through the reading and preaching of the Bible, God speaks to his people. Like the Roman soldier Cornelius, God's people are blessed when they come together expecting to receive a word from God.

Acts 10:33 **"Now we are all here in the presence of God to listen to everything the Lord has commanded you to tell us."**

Responding in song

Inevitably as we hear God speak, we want to respond in praise. Down through the ages God's people have used a variety of worship styles to sing their praises.

Colossians 3:16 **Let the word of Christ dwell in you richly as you teach and admonish one another with all wisdom, and as you sing psalms, hymns and spiritual songs with gratitude in your hearts to God.**

Bringing our prayers

An important part of worship is the intercessions, when in prayer we bring before God the needs both of the church and of the world. Inter-

1 Timothy 2:1-2 **I urge, then, first of all, that requests, prayers, intercession and thanksgiving be made for every-**

one - for kings and all those in authority, that we may live peaceful and quiet lives in all godliness and holiness.

1 Corinthians 11:23-26 For I received from the Lord what I also passed on to you: The Lord Jesus, on the night he was betrayed, took bread, and when he had given thanks, he broke it and said, "This is my body, which is for you; do this in remembrance of me." In the same way, after supper he took the cup, saying, "This cup is the new covenant in my blood; do this, whenever you drink it, in remembrance of me." For whenever you eat this bread and drink this cup, you proclaim the Lord's death until he comes.

1 Corinthians 11:27-28 Therefore, whoever eats the bread or drinks the cup of the Lord in an unworthy manner will be guilty of sinning against the body and blood of the Lord. A man ought to examine himself before he eats of the bread and drinks of the cup.

cession is in fact an expression of our love for others. Not to pray is not to love.

Remembering the Lord Jesus

Christian worship climaxes in the celebration of the Lord's Supper. Here we remember not only that Jesus died for us, but also that he rose again and is with us now. We also look forward to the day when Jesus shall return again in glory and shall establish his kingdom for ever and ever.

Expressing our fellowship with one another

The Lord's Supper is by definition a communal act. As we come to the communion table, we come together. It is here that we sense our unity with one another - here we pray for one another. It is vital that we are right with one another.

Renewing our vows

Whenever the Lord's Supper is meaningful, it will end in renewed dedication to the service of God. This is the moment when we may renew our baptismal vows of love and loyalty to our Lord.

Psalm 116:12-14 **How can I repay the Lord for all his goodness to me? I will lift up the cup of salvation and call on the name of the Lord. I will fulfil my vows to the Lord in the presence of all his people.**

Memory verses: Psalm 116:12-14

LIVING TOGETHER IN CHRIST

Belonging to one another

1 Corinthians 12:25-27 [All the] parts [of the body] should have equal concern for each other. If one part suffers, every part suffers with it; if one part is honoured, every part rejoices with it. Now you are the body of Christ, and each one of you is a part of it.

When we are born again, we are born into a family. We belong to one another. And because we belong to one another, we have a responsibility for one another. Church membership in the first place is about commitment to one another.

Loving one another

John 13:34-35 "A new command I give you: Love one another. As I have loved you, so you must love one another. By this all men will know that you are my disciples, if you love one another."

Love is more than a feeling. Love if it is to be real must be expressed. Jesus washed his disciples' feet, and then went on to give his life for them on a cross. Jesus calls us to be equally down-to-earth in our loving. Others must see the difference, if they are to believe.

Greeting one another

Romans 16:15-16 Greet Philologus, Julia, Nereus and his sister, and Olympas and all the saints with them. Greet one another with a holy kiss.

Greeting one another involves more than saying hello. It involves more than showing physical affection. It involves knowing the name of the other - knowing the situation of the other. Love must always have a cutting edge.

Encouraging one another

1 Thessalonians 5:11 Encourage one another and build each other up.

Few of us remain on a perpetual even keel. We all have our ups and

19

downs. We all need encouragement. Encouragement is actually vital for personal growth and development. Children, for instance, who are encouraged at home and at school often do well in life. The same is true in the Christian family. Don't forget that encouragement can also be expressed in actions as well as in words!

Bearing one another's burdens

In cases where Christians badly fail their Lord and discipline is necessary, restoration should always be in view. There is no place for judgmentalism. Rather we are to draw alongside and bring help. What is true of the 'burden' of failure, is also to be true of other 'burdens' in life. God does not intend us to grin and bear it alone.

Galatians 6:1-2 **Brothers, if someone is caught in a sin, you who are spiritual should restore him gently. But watch yourself, or you also may be tempted. Carry each other's burdens, and in this way you will fulfil the law of Christ.**

Praying for one another

All of us need prayer, because all of us in one way or another need God's healing touch in our lives. We may not necessarily be physically sick, but instead we may be spiritually 'below par'. If, however, we are to be blessed by the prayers of others, then we must be open about our needs

James 5:16 **Therefore confess your sins to each other and pray for each other so that you may be healed.**

1 Samuale 18:3; 23:15, 16
Jonathan made a covenant with David because he loved him as himself ... While David was at Horesh in the Desert of Ziph, he learned that Saul had come out to take his life. And Saul's son Jonathan went to David at Horesh and helped him to find strength in God.

Covenanting together

Sometimes church membership is described as entering into a 'covenant' with one another. A covenant may be likened to a binding agreement or contract. When we welcome others into church membership we are formally committing ourselves to love one another and stand by one another whatever the cost.

Memory verse: John 13:34-35

LIVING TOGETHER UNDER THE LORDSHIP OF CHRIST

Jesus is Lord of his church

Some churches are governed by bishops, others through elders or through church councils. For Baptists it is the church meeting which is the ultimate authority in their life together. Yet when Baptists come together in church meeting they are concerned to engage not in in a form of democracy ('government by the people for the people') but rather in a form of theocracy ('God ruling through the church meeting'). Jesus is to be lord of his church.

Colossians 1:18 **And he is the head of the body ... so that in everything he might have the supremacy.**

Appointing leaders

When the first 'deacons' were appointed, it was left to the church - and not to the apostles - to choose seven men. The church meeting continues to be the place where leaders are appointed.

Acts 6:3, 5-6 **"Brothers, choose seven men from among you who are known to be full of the Spirit and wisdom" ... His proposal pleased the whole group. They chose Stephen, a man full of faith and of the Holy Spirit; also Philip, Procorus, Nicanor, Timon, Parmenas, and Nicolas from Antioch, a convert to Judaism. They presented these men to the apostles, who prayed and laid their hands on them.**

Administering finance

When a particular financial need was made known to the church, the

Acts 11:29-30 **The disciples, each according to his ability,** decided to provide help for the brothers living in Judea. This they did, sending their gift to the elders by Barnabas and Saul.

Acts 15:22 **Then the apostles and elders, with the whole church, decided.**

Matthew 18:15-17 **"If your brother sins against you, go and show him his fault, just between the two of you. If he listens to you, you have won your brother over. But if he will not listen, take one or two others along, so that 'every matter may be established by the testimony of two or three witnesses.' If he refuses to listen to them, tell it to the church; and if he refuses to listen even to the church, treat him as you would a pagan or a tax collector."**

disciples - and not the elders alone - were involved in the decision - making process. The church meeting continues to be the place where budgets are approved.

Admitting members

At an early period in its life the early church was faced with the question of admitting members from a non-Jewish background. Although the apostles and the elders took the initiative in thrashing the matter through, the church as a whole was involved in making the decision to welcome Gentile believers into their midst. The church meeting continues to be the place where membership matters are decided.

Exercising discipline

Jesus makes clear that the ultimate recourse in discipline is not to the church's leaders, but to the church itself. When all else fails, the church meeting has the final authority.

Honouring leaders

The New Testament concept of the church meeting does not rule out the need for leaders. Leadership is part of the God-given task of those who preach and teach.

1 Timothy 5:17 **The elders who direct the affairs of the church well are worthy of double honour, especially those whose work is preaching and teaching.**

Submitting to leaders

The church delegates some of its authority to leaders, authority which the leaders are free to use until the church withdraws its recognition of them. Good leadership has always the well-being of the church in view.

Hebrews 13:17 **Obey your leaders and submit to their authority. They keep watch over you as men who must give an account. Obey them so that their work will be a joy, not a burden, for that would be of no advantage to you.**

Memory verse: Colossians 1:18

SERVING CHRIST

Romans 12:6-8 We have different gifts, according to the grace given us. If a man's gift is prophesying, let him use it in proportion to his faith. If it is serving, let him serve; if it is teaching, let him teach; if it is encouraging, let him encourage; if it is contributing to the needs of others, let him give generously; if it is leadership, let him govern diligently; if it is showing mercy, let him do it cheerfully.

1 Corinthians 12:7-11 Now to each one the manifestation of the Spirit is given for the common good. To one there is given through the Spirit the message of wisdom, to another the message of knowledge by means of the same Spirit, to another faith by the same Spirit, to another gifts of healing by that one Spirit, to another miraculous powers, to another prophecy, to another distinguishing between spirits, to another speaking in different kinds of tongues, and to still another the interpretation of tongues. All these are the

Discovering our gifts

Everybody is gifted! What is more we all vary in the gifts we have been given. Our task is to discover our gifts and then, by God's grace, to develop them in his service.

Using our gifts for the good of others

God does not give gifts to make us feel good about ourselves - but rather to enable us to serve others. Precisely how we serve will vary from situation to situation.

Serving beyond the church

A key role for those gifted with leadership in the church is to equip God's people to serve in the world. In other words, it is not so much a question of the members supporting the leaders in their particular sphere of service, but rather of the leaders supporting the members in the work to which God has called and gifted them!

Serving in the wider community

In the ancient world salt not only gave flavour, it also acted as a preservative. In other words Jesus expects his disciples to exercise an antiseptic influence and be a positive influence for good.

Serving through good time management

Time is a precious gift from God. All of us are to be good managers of our time. There are various ways of wasting time. We can waste time, for instance, by failing to distinguish the important from the urgent.

work of one and the same Spirit, and he gives them to each one, just as he determines.

Ephesians 4:11-12 It was he who gave some to be apostles, some to be prophets, some to be evangelists, and some to be pastors and teachers, to prepare God's people for works of service.

Matthew 5:13 "You are the salt of the earth".

Ephesians 5:15-16 Be very careful, then, how you live - not as unwise but as wise, making the most of every opportunity ...

Serving through giving

2 Corinthians 9:6-8 **Remember this: Whoever sows sparingly will also reap sparingly, and whoever sows generously will also reap generously. Each man should give what he has decided in his heart to give, not reluctantly or under compulsion, for God loves a cheerful giver. And God is able to make all grace abound to you, so that in all things at all times, having all that you need, you will abound in every good work.**

Money too is a gift from God. Therefore we need to think carefully on how we manage our financial resources - and then give generously.

Serving through proportionate giving

1 Corinthians 16:2 **On the first day of every week, each one of you should set aside a sum of money in keeping with his income.**

In the Christian church there are no membership dues. Rather we are called to give a realistic proportion of our income. A tenth is often a good guide - but remember, God sees not just what we give, but also what we keep for ourselves. For some Christians a double-tithe might even be appropriate!

Memory verse: Matthew 5:13

WITNESSING TO CHRIST

Witnessing where we are

Witnessing to Jesus begins right where we are - the place where we live, work, study and play. It is in our 'Jerusalems' where we can often be the most effective.

Acts 1:8 **"You will receive power when the Holy Spirit comes on you; and you will be my witnesses in Jerusalem, and in all Judea and Samaria, and to the ends of the earth."**

Telling our story

Witnessing involves telling others about what Jesus has done for us - and what he means for us now. Not everybody may have a dramatic story to share, but everybody can speak of the difference Jesus makes to life! There's a lot to be said for writing down our story and sharing it with a friend to ensure that it is jargon-free and to the point.

John 9:25 **"One thing I do know. I was blind but now I see!"**

Being at the ready

Witnessing normally involves responding to opportunities which are given to us. Brashness does the Christian cause no favours. There is a time to be silent, but also a time not to be silent.

1 Peter 3:15 **Always be prepared to give an answer to everyone who asks you to give the reason for the hope that you have. But do this with gentleness and respect.**

Making friends for Jesus

Effective witnessing involves making friends with people outside

Matthew 11:19 **"The Son of Man came eating and drinking,** and they say, 'Here is a glutton and a drunkard, a friend of tax collectors and "sinners".'"

Luke 5:27-29 **Jesus ... saw a tax collector by the name of Levi sitting at his tax booth. "Follow me," Jesus said to him, and Levi got up, left everything and followed him. Then Levi held a great banquet for Jesus at his house, and a large crowd of tax collectors and others were eating with them.**

Mark 5:19 **Jesus did not let him, but said, "Go home to your family [literally: 'your own': ie your family, your friends, your circle of acquaintances] and tell them how much the Lord has done for you, and how he has had mercy on you."**

the church. Unfortunately the older we grow in our Christian faith, the more we are tempted to live our lives in a Christian ghetto. Jesus deliberately rubbed shoulders with non-religious people - and so should we.

Inviting people home

Effective witnessing usually entails inviting people into our homes before we invite them to our church. It is within the context of the home that people will hopefully sense our normality - and also our faith! Friendship evangelism takes time, but can also be very fruitful.

Networking for Jesus

Bridges of friendship are often built as we make the most of our network of relationships. Most of us link into at least four distinct areas of relationships:

- the family (eg parents, spouse, children, brothers and sisters)
- work (eg the boss, our colleagues) or school (fellow students & teachers)
- leisure (eg football team, sports' club)
- general social contacts (eg neighbours).

Here are people to befriend - and bring to Jesus. It's helpful to make a list of all those who fall into these categories - and then pray that God will give us an opportunity to share the good news of Jesus with them.

Going out on a limb for Jesus

Witnessing takes many and varied forms. What may be right for one person, may be wrong for another. We need to be imaginative, but also sensitive, to each and every situation.

1 Corinthians 9:22 **To the weak I became weak, to win the weak. I have become all things to all men so that by all possible means I might save some.**

Memory Verse: 1 Peter 3:15

EXPRESSING CHRIST'S LOVE TO OTHERS

Bringing in the kingdom

Matthew 11:2-5 John [the Baptist] ... sent his disciples to ask him, "Are you the one who was to come, or should we expect someone else?" Jesus replied, "Go back and report to John what you hear and see: The blind receive sight, the lame walk, those who have leprosy are cured, the deaf hear, the dead are raised, and the good news is preached to the poor."

The kingdom of God is not so much an area, but God in action. Jesus not only proclaimed the coming of the kingdom of God, he also demonstrated the kingdom in action as he transformed people's lives. Indeed, the very 'signs' of the kingdom confirmed the truth of his claims. So also today kingdom action must accompany kingdom preaching if the gospel is to be good news to the poor. Here is the basis not only for social service but also for political action.

Caring for the needy

Matthew 25:35-36, 40 "I was hungry and you gave me something to eat, I was thirsty and you gave me something to drink, I was a stranger and you invited me in, I needed clothes and you clothed me, I was sick and you looked after me, I was in prison and you came to visit me ... I tell you the truth, whatever you did for one of the least of these brothers of mine, you did for me."

At the end of time when Christ sits in judgement on the nations of the world, he will welcome into his kingdom those who have shown practical love to those in need. Note too that no one is too insignificant to be the object of our care.

Loving the stranger

Luke 10:33-34, 36-37 "But a Samaritan, as he travelled, came

Love for our neighbour means that we cannot pass by on the other side in the face of need. It also means that we can never restrict love to our own kind. Love knows no ethnic, cultural or religious boundaries.

where the man was; and when he saw him, he took pity on him. He went to him and bandaged his wounds, pouring on oil and wine. Then he put the man on his own donkey, brought him to an inn and took care of him ... Which of these three do you think was a neighbour to the man who fell into the hands of robbers?" The expert in the law replied, "The one who had mercy on him." Jesus told him, "Go and do likewise."

Helping the poor

Where there is no social conscience, there God's love is not present. Just as there was no limit to the concern of Jesus for our need, so too there should be no limit to our concern for those less privileged than ourselves.

1 John 3:16-17   This is how we know what love is: Jesus Christ laid down his life for us. And we ought to lay down our lives for our brothers. If anyone has material possessions and sees his brother in need but has no pity on him, how can the love of God be in him?

Acting the peacemaker

Peacemaking is more than smoothing over ruffled feathers; rather it is concerned to establish relationships that are right because they are rooted in righteousness. Peacemaking is not about compromises - it is about dealing with the root causes of those things which divide us.

Matthew 5:9   "Blessed are the peacemakers, for they will be called sons of God."

John 20:21 Jesus said, "As the Father has sent me, I am sending you."

Going the Jesus way

Jesus not only preached good news - he was good news. He fed the hungry and healed the sick. The love of God was 'made flesh'. To go the way of Jesus is to be involved in 'holistic mission', caring for bodies as well as souls.

> *Memory verse: John 20:21*

BELONGING TO THE WIDER FAMILY OF CHRIST

Christians ...

When we are baptised we are joining the world-wide family of God. In Jesus all barriers of race and gender, social standing and church background, are overcome. True, distinctions still remain - but they no longer count.

Galatians 3:26-28 **You are all sons of God through faith in Christ Jesus, for all of you who were baptised into Christ have clothed yourselves with Christ. There is neither Jew nor Greek, slave nor free, male nor female, for you are all one in Christ Jesus.**

... and Baptist Christians

When we become a church member, we join that part of the family of God called 'Baptist'. It's the largest Protestant family in the world - with some 37 million baptised members. Baptists believe that their way of being the church is not just one of several options open to them - rather their study of God's Word leads them to believe that this is God's way for living their life together. The Baptist way of being the church includes:

Confessing the faith

Baptists practise believers' baptism. At the end of the day the emphasis is not on the quantity of water, but rather on the quality of faith. Baptism expresses the believer's response of faith to the grace of God.

Acts 22:16 **"And now what are you waiting for? Get up, be baptised and wash your sins away, calling on his name".**

Acts 2:41-42 Those who accepted his message were baptised, and about three thousand were added to their number that day. They devoted themselves to the apostles' teaching and to the fellowship, to the breaking of bread and to prayer.

Acts 13:1-3 In the church at Antioch there were prophets and teachers: Barnabas, Simeon called Niger, Lucius of Cyrene, Manaen (who had been brought up with Herod the tetrarch) and Saul. While they were worshipping the Lord and fasting, the Holy Spirit said, "Set apart for me Barnabas and Saul for the work to which I have called them." So after they had fasted and prayed, they placed their hands on them and sent them off.

Ephesians 4:4-6 There is one body and one Spirit - just as you were called to one hope when you were called - one Lord, one faith, one baptism; one God and Father of all, who is over all and through all and in all.

Living together in community

Along with believers' baptism is the Baptist emphasis on a church as a body of committed believers. For Baptists the church is a local community of believers, gathered together out of the world, who have committed themselves to Christ and to one another.

Living under the lordship of Christ

The local church is where the heart of Baptist life is. Baptists adopt a congregational system of church government, believing that God rules through church meetings made up of members of a local church. Each Baptist church therefore is self-governing.

Associating with others

In spite of their emphasis on the local church, Baptists believe not in independency but inter-dependency. Just as no individual Christian can afford to be a loner, neither can any local church go it alone.

Serving one another

From their beginnings Baptists have treasured the Reformation principle of 'the priesthood of all believers'. Baptists believe that all God's people have equal access to God and in turn have equal responsibility to serve God.

1 Peter 2:9 **But you are a chosen people, a royal priesthood, a holy nation, a people belonging to God, that you may declare the praises of him who called you out of darkness into his wonderful light.**

Sharing the Faith

Baptists have been characterised by a passion for the gospel. Indeed, their rite of believers' baptism emphasises the necessity of conversion.

2 Corinthians 5:20 **We are therefore Christ's ambassadors, as though God were making his appeal through us. We implore you on Christ's behalf: Be reconciled to God.**

Memory verses: Ephesians 4:4-6